presented to

....

from

....

on this date

....

wisdom for women

CAROL L. FITZPATRICK

A DayMaker Greeting Book

Woman was lovingly and uniquely created by God to be not only a helpmate to man, but to have her own special influence upon the earth. I must admit, I didn't always see my own life this way.

When I was young, women were seen only in the "shadow of man." While we married for love, marriage was clearly expected of us, perhaps before we'd even pursued a career. And then we had families.

Only when I came to Christ, in a Christian commitment of faith, did I finally realize the importance of being a woman. All of the talents and resources God has built into each of us are essential——to love a husband, maintain a home, nurture children so they exhibit godly behavior, and perform specific tasks here on earth (Ephesians 2:10).

My hope is that, in this little book of devotions, you'll come to know how much God loves you and, at the same time, gain a better understanding of yourself as a woman.

As we journey together, perhaps I'll even touch your heart. If so, it is simply because the powerful Word of God has embraced my own so profoundly.

——Carol L. Fitzpatrick

vocalizing a prayer

And when you are praying, do not use meaningless
repetition, as the Gentiles do, for they suppose that they
will be heard for their many words. Matthew 6:7

Remember kneeling beside your bed and praying when you were a kid? Why did it all seem so simple then? We just talked to God like He was really there and kept our requests short and simple.

Then, as you got older, the lengthy and spiritual prayers of the "older saints" became intimidating. So, where's the balance? Reading a little further in this passage from Matthew, at verse 9, Jesus gives us His own example for prayer. If you can remember the acrostic ACTS, you'll have an excellent formula for prayer: Adoration, Confession, Thanksgiving, and Supplication.

As we come before the Lord we first need to honor Him as Creator, Master, Savior, and Lord. Reflect on who He is and praise Him. And because we're human we need to confess and repent of our daily sins. Following this we should be in a mode of thanksgiving. Finally, our prayer requests should be upheld. My usual order for requests is self, family members, and life's pressing issues. Keeping a prayer journal allows for a written record of God's answers.

Your prayers certainly don't have to be elaborate or polished. God does not judge your way with words. He knows your heart. He wants to hear from You.

{ P R A Y E R }

Lord, Your Word says that my prayers rise up to heaven like incense from the earth. Remind me daily to send a sweet savor Your way!

king forever and ever

The Lord is King forever and ever;
Nations have perished from His land. Psalm 10:16

When my sisters and I were young we lived in a huge, newly built, custom home. My father's pride and joy, as a part-time carpenter, was the gleaming oak staircase going to the upstairs.

One day several of us got into a fight over who should have control of a bottle of india ink. As one sister attempted to carry the glass container downstairs for a parental pronouncement, another sister knocked it from her hands. The bottle crashed down the stairway, its thick black ink cascading furiously all the way to the first floor.

My father looked as if he were going to have a stroke when he saw the mess. During the next few years he tried everything to eradicate those angry stains but nothing would take them away short of rebuilding the entire staircase.

Satan, whose dominion is the world, has devoted all his efforts to eradicating Christianity. Yet, while the evil one's influence can seem as ugly as any ink stain, Satan's mark on this earth will not be permanent. The reason? God's Son,

Jesus Christ, lives forever within those who call upon His name. And despite the efforts of the evil one, Jesus will remain King and will one day soon come back to claim this earth for His own, forever and ever.

Are you assured of your place in Christ's kingdom?

{ PRAYER }

Lord, as this world becomes increasingly evil, reflecting the one who holds its "title deed," remind me that You're coming back to claim all that is rightfully Yours.

our advocate and defender

"Every one therefore who shall confess Me before men,
I will also confess him before My Father who is in heaven.
But whoever shall deny Me before men, I will also deny him
before My Father who is in heaven." Matthew 10:32-33

My sisters and I attended private schools for most of our lives but that did not render us immune to rowdies or bullies. And since we walked a few miles to school each day, we were at times easy prey.

Busy with friends her own age, my older sister didn't usually accompany my younger sister and me on our morning trek.

However, when we returned home one day relating that two big kids from the nearby public school had threatened to beat us up the next day, she rallied to the cause. As she instructed, we traversed our normal route while she lagged watchfully a short distance behind.

Suddenly the two boys jumped out of the bushes ahead. And just like a superwoman, our sister pounced on them, easily overpowering both and giving them bloody noses in the process. I'll never forget that scene as long as I live. It felt so incredible to have an invincible defender!

If we know Jesus Christ and have responded to His invitation to receive Him as Savior, Jesus remains forever our advocate before the Father, saying with love, "She's mine." Know that you are so precious to Jesus that He gave His life for you. Doesn't it feel incredible to have Jesus as your defender?

{ P R A Y E R }

Lord, how reassuring it is to know
You mightily defend not only my body
but my soul against attack.

remember the sabbath

"Remember the Sabbath day, to keep it holy.
Six days you shall labor and do all your work, but the seventh day
is a Sabbath of the Lord your God; in it you shall not do any work. . . .
For in six days the Lord made the heavens and the earth, the sea and
all that is in them, and rested on the seventh day." Exodus 20:8-11

During the 1950s in Missouri, where I grew up, blue laws virtually shut down the city on Sundays. You could see whole families, dressed in their Sunday best, walking toward the nearest big intersection, where you'd find a different denomination on each corner. The rest of the day might be spent enjoying picnics, bike rides, or "visiting Grandma." I loved those relaxing times with the extended family.

Merchants finally managed to get these laws overturned and the stores opened on Sunday. Sales were timed to begin early on the Sabbath, enticing people to make a choice between church and shopping. On a Sunday morning compare the number of parked cars in the mall with those in the church lots. This worldly strategy has certainly been effective.

In the very beginning of our marriage my husband and I made a decision to honor God on Sunday. He has blessed our family over and over for this faithful

commitment, providing not only the weekly spiritual guidance we desperately need,

but also giving our bodies and souls the rest they require.

{ P R A Y E R }

Lord, please help me to remember that
Your commandments are always for my good.

true love means sacrifice

And they spat on Him, and took the reed and began to beat Him
on the head. And after they had mocked Him, they took His robe off
and put His garments on Him, and led Him away to crucify Him.

Matthew 27:30-31

Years ago the popular movie *Love Story* coined the unforgettable phrase, "Love means never having to say you're sorry." What a fallacy, and more is the pity for those who bought into this lie! For love demands that we always say we're sorry. How else can relationships be restored?

Those two words, "I'm sorry," have the power to keep families and churches together. I once knew a pastor whose refusal to recognize his humanity caused almost half of the church family to seek membership elsewhere. In his eyes he had done nothing wrong, but what harm would have been done to admit the possibility of poor judgment?

To admit fallibility is to make a sacrifice. To have done nothing wrong and to offer the ultimate sacrifice is an act only possible by God's Son. Jesus' offering of His body at Calvary gave eternal life to all who believe in Him.

Is there someone from whom you are estranged who is waiting to hear those two little words? Say you're sorry.

{ PRAYER }

Lord, You sacrificed all You had to provide my eternal salvation.
Help me today to express true sorrow for my sins.

walking in the light

The fear of the Lord prolongs life,
But the years of the wicked will be shortened.
The hope of the righteous is gladness,
But the expectation of the wicked perishes.
The way of the Lord is a stronghold to the upright,
But ruin to the workers of iniquity.
The righteous will never be shaken,
but the wicked will not dwell in the land.
Proverbs 10:27-30

Instead of being a cause of terror in our hearts, that phrase, "fear of the Lord," means to reverence and honor Him as God. For He alone is God, righteous, and wise enough to intervene and effect positive changes in our lives. Instilling this truth in our children enables them to know the ways of the Lord.

Knowing that everything which emanates from God is good enables us to trust Him in every crisis and walk in His ways. Because in each situation there are two alternative reactions. On the one hand exists the opportunity to act honorably, and on the other freedom to disobey. The choice is entirely ours.

God's very nature is goodness. Therefore, everything which stems from

Him reflects His character. This knowledge should cause hope to flood our lives. Unshaken by the winds of change, then we can stand firm in the face of any kind of adversity, like a boat anchored to its strong moorings.

Obedience always brings inner peace, contentment, and happiness, while stepping out from underneath God's umbrella of protection only gets us soaked and saturated with sin.

{ PRAYER }

Lord, show us how to raise children who reflect
the goodness of Your character!

where do you take refuge?

Be gracious, O God, for man has trampled upon me;
Fighting all day long he oppresses me.
My foes have trampled upon me all day long,
For they are many who fight proudly against me.
When I am afraid, I will put my trust in Thee.
In God, whose word I praise, In God I have put my trust;
I shall not be afraid. What can mere man do to me?

Psalm 56:1-4

When my father was away during World War II, my mom, sister, and I lived with my grandparents. At the time I was only three years old or so. Frequently, I'd hide under their long, wooden porch, making my world a little smaller, I suppose. Looking out through the latticed covering, somehow I felt safe.

David wrote this psalm when the Philistines had seized him in Gath. These Philistines had been enemies of the Israelites for a long time. At one point they'd even stolen the ark of the covenant. They'd probably never forgiven David for killing their giant, Goliath. I wonder if David reflected during his present predicament, remembering the time in his youth when he'd faced that giant with only five smooth stones and a sling. He had called upon his God to deliver him, and the Lord had prevailed (1 Samuel 17:37-50).

Where do you go for refuge? I run to the arms of my loving Father, just as David did in his own crisis. And He always comes through.

{ PRAYER }
O Lord, You alone are my refuge and strength.
Help me to come to You first in a crisis.

retreat to a quiet place
from the cares of the day
to a place of meditation–
a place where you can pray

a father to the fatherless

A father of the fatherless and a judge for the widows,
Is God in His holy habitation. Psalm 68:5

Between the rising divorce rate and those who have chosen to birth children without benefit of marriage, over half of the households in America have become fatherless. The Christian men's movement, Promise Keepers, has sought to rectify this tragedy by calling men to refocus their priorities, first on God and then on their families.

But what about the moms? What can we do to insure that our children aren't among the fatherless? We can make sure that we are fully committed to the Lord. If you're holding down a full-time job, finding the time for Bible study and devotions is a gigantic challenge. It's up to you to get inventive.

Perhaps you can teach the children how to make their own lunches——and use that extra fifteen minutes to read the Word. This is an investment in their future growth: As you learn, so will your children.

If divorce has touched you personally, all that anger, hurt, and pain must be dealt with so that your children don't feel desolate. It's hard enough for them to lose one parent through absence, let alone the other to hostility or depression.

God has promised to be "a father to the fatherless." Count on Him to keep His Word. And instead of attempting to be both father and mother, you can just be a mom to your kids.

{ PRAYER }

Lord, life seems like such a futile uphill climb sometimes.
Help me to entrust all my heavy burdens to Your care.

martha and mary

A woman named Martha welcomed Him into her home. And she had
a sister called Mary, who moreover was listening to the Lord's word,
seated at His feet. But Martha was distracted with all her preparations;
and she came up to Him, and said, "Lord, do You not care that my sister
has left me to do all the serving alone? Then tell her to help me."
Luke 10:38-40

Isn't this just how we feel when the men in our household excuse themselves from the table as soon as the first dirty dish appears? Martha, ever the perfect hostess, was left to do all the work. It didn't seem fair.

However, what Martha really desired was a release from her compulsive neatness. And that's when the Lord presented her with a process for "chilling out."

" 'Martha, Martha, you are worried and bothered about so many things; but only a few things are necessary, really only one, for Mary has chosen the good part, which shall not be taken away from her' " (Luke 10:41-42). In other words, all the busyness which now preoccupied Martha didn't really matter. Jesus was here and she was passing up a tremendous opportunity to learn from Him.

After all, who knew better than Christ how to put the pressures of life into perspective? He had only three years in which to establish His ministry, train up His disciples, and present the Gospel. Yet we see no record of Him hurrying others or running at a frantic pace.

Have you taken time to get to know your Lord? Perhaps your life, like Martha's, is missing the best part.

{ PRAYER }
Lord, I pray for peace today
from my busy schedule
so I may learn at Your knee.

rebuke the sinner

"Be on your guard! If your brother sins, rebuke him;
and if he repents, forgive him." Luke 17:3

Back in the 1950s, neighborhood accountability was a fact of life. Families took pride in raising their children properly. And on the rare occasion when someone's kid did act up, it was guaranteed that by suppertime the parents would already have heard about it through the neighborhood grapevine. Punishment was swift and commensurate with the crime.

Since my husband and I had both benefited from the same kind of environment, we agreed completely on how we'd raise our children. However, in the early 1970s, we realized that a whole new breed of parents had evolved. They lacked the faith and fortitude to be disciplined or to discipline their own children.

Their children grew up for the most part without spiritual guidance, morality, or goals.

It still takes the knowledge of Jesus Christ to redeem our world. Here Jesus admonished his disciples to "rebuke" their brothers if they've sinned. Why?

Because sin is a progressive fall. And "real love" means intervening that we might get back on track.

Have you shared your love of Jesus with a neighbor? Pray today that God might open a door or window to your witness.

{ P R A Y E R }

Lord, give me the courage to be honest
so that children can experience the safety
and security of proper boundaries.

he dwelt among us

And the Word became flesh, and dwelt among us, and we saw His glory, glory as of the only begotten from the Father, full of grace and truth. . . . No one has seen God at any time; the only begotten God, who is in the bosom of the Father, He has explained Him. John 1:14, 18

That phrase, "dwelt among us," means God took on the form of a human body, leaving the peace, security, and hope of heaven, and came to earth to become a model for men and women.

How do you teach children not to lie, cheat, or steal? By being an example before them of proper behavior. Jesus showed us by example what it means to lead a perfect life, despite the evil surrounding Him. "For we do not have a high priest who cannot sympathize with our weaknesses, but one who has been tempted in all things as we are, yet without sin" (Hebrews 4:15).

When Satan bombarded Christ during an intense time of temptation in the wilderness, Christ showed us how to repel such attacks successfully: through liberal use of the Word of God, prayer, and obedience.

Blaming Adam for initiating humans into the vicious cycle of sin doesn't get any of us off the hook. It's our nature to sin. And that's why we need a new nature. This is exactly what Christ purchased for us on Calvary's cross, the right to be indwelt with the very Spirit of God. A fresh start, isn't that what all of us are seeking?

{ P R A Y E R }
Lord, strengthen my faith today.
Help me to overcome
the evil one's daily temptations.

protection for widows

The Lord will tear down the house of the proud,
But He will establish the boundary of the widow. Proverbs 15:25

Christmas shopping preoccupied my father's thoughts as he picked out one special gift for each child, something he or she had wanted all year. But just after the last gift had been purchased, a severe heart attack overtook my dad. Although he was rushed to the hospital adjacent to the shopping center, he died almost immediately.

My mother's first concern was how she might continue caring for her children, all ten of whom lived at home.

Although she hadn't worked outside the home in years, Mom donned a beret and smock and began selling pastel portraits at the local swap meet.

Eventually Mom also filled artists' chairs at Knotts Berry Farm and the Movieland Wax Museum. Her beautiful pastel portraits still hang in homes throughout our area. And the friendships she made with other artists endure to this day.

No matter what her hardships, Mom has honored God, in whom she placed her faith and the care of her life. She's now been widowed far longer than the years she was married. She's raised her children, paid off her mortgage, and passed down her love of art to all her grandchildren.

seek wisdom, not self

When a wicked man comes, contempt also comes,
And with dishonor comes reproach. Proverbs 18:3

The delightful movie *Doctor Doolittle* presented a magical animal called the "Push me, pull you." Such is the woman who has a divided heart! She can never truly go forward in life.

One young woman whom I counseled certainly fit this description. She'd fallen in love with a worthless wretch of a man and become convinced that she somehow possessed the power to change him. Not only could she not change him, she was also unable to raise her children properly. Because this mother was emotionally paralyzed, her children never received godly examples of faith, integrity, and stability.

Women become vulnerable the instant truth is replaced with desire. It's like when the tip of an arrow finds the one small point of vulnerability and penetrates a suit of armor.

So how can we teach our daughters to be wise? By acquiring knowledge ourselves. As we study and store God's Word in times of peace, our first thoughts during periods of stress or crisis will be Scripture. People falter because they fail to plan. If we just do what God expects of us, despite the magnetic pull of sin, we gain strength of character. Negotiating with evil nets us a zero every time.

{ PRAYER }

Lord, sometimes I want so badly to be loved
that I trust the wrong people.
Please guide me to those
who are trustworthy.

search for happiness

I said to myself, "Come now, I will test you with pleasure. So enjoy yourself."
And behold, it too was futility. I explored with my mind how to stimulate my body
with wine while my mind was guiding me wisely, and how to take hold of folly,
until I could see what good there is for the sons of men to do under heaven
the few years of their lives. Ecclesiastes 2:1-3

Ah, the endless search for happiness. Remember when you thought that new dress or outfit would bring you happiness? And it did until you wore it again and again. Then you moved on to bigger and better things, like a brand-new car or a twenty-five-hundred-square-foot house or a summer home. . . .

Solomon explored with his mind how to stimulate his body. Then he enlarged his empire, built houses, planted vineyards, made gardens and parks, engineered ponds of water to irrigate a forest, bought male and female slaves, flocks and herds, and collected silver and gold. All that his eyes desired he achieved. But did any of this bring him true happiness?

"Thus I considered all my activities which my hands had done and the labor which I had exerted, and behold all was vanity and striving after wind and there was no profit under the sun" (Ecclesiastes 2:11). It finally occurred to Solomon that in the end he would die and leave it all to others who followed him.

{ PRAYER }

Lord, help me not to be drawn away from You
by the endless pursuit of things.
Instead, I desire Your presence, guidance, and wisdom.

the days of your youth

Remember also your Creator in the days of your youth,
before the evil days come and the years draw near when you will say,
"I have no delight in them." Fear God and keep His commandments, because this
applies to every person. God will bring every act to judgment, everything which is
hidden, whether it is good or evil. Ecclesiastes 12:1, 13-14

Most of us have encountered women who freely share biblical truths "handed down to them" from their grandmothers or mothers. Is the faith being displayed in their lives?

The Book of Ecclesiastes concludes with the admonition not only to remember our Creator when we are young, but to continue following His precepts throughout our time on earth. For nothing is sadder than to see those who began the race of life with so much vigor and potential now sitting on the sidelines watching the parade pass by.

High school reunions are great places to witness such scenes. Those girls whose faces glowed with extraordinary promise at eighteen may now display ones that appear more like a map of New York City. They've been betrayed, besieged, and bewildered by people promising much and delivering little.

Have you forgotten the God of your youth? Have His principles been compromised away by the pressures of a world that teaches the Ten Commandments are optional? With the Lord's help, it's not too late to turn it all around.

{ PRAYER }

Lord, if I look back and see a trail of regret,
please give me the courage to change the view.

arise in the morning
sing praise to the king
give thanks for the beauty
that each day brings

an intimate conversation

"And this is eternal life, that they may know Thee,
the only true God, and Jesus Christ whom Thou has sent.
I glorified Thee on earth, having accomplished the work
which Thou hast given Me to do. And now, glorify Thou Me
together with Thyself, Father, with the glory which I had
with Thee before the world was." John 17:3-5

Have you ever unwittingly overheard an intimate conversation? Well, that's exactly what this chapter of John is like. We are privileged to overhear Jesus as He speaks to the Father.

Christ was with the Father before the world was. That makes Him not only eternal but equal with the Father. These are the claims Jesus made to the Pharisees who constantly confronted Him concerning His origin.

Christ's prayer to the Father also includes concern for whom the Father has given to Him. " 'I manifested Thy name to the men whom Thou gavest Me out of the world; Thine they were, and Thou gavest them to Me, and they have kept Thy Word' " (John 17:6). Notice that these are the people who respond to God's message and keep His Word.

Then Jesus also asks the Father to keep us in His name. " 'Holy Father, keep them in Thy name, the name which Thou has given Me, that they may be one, even as We are' " (John 17:11). Christ prayed that God's power would keep us from being swayed by the world and the evil one (John 17:15).

{ PRAYER }

Lord Jesus Christ, I acknowledge You as God and Savior.

a true mother's love

"And now, O Lord my God, Thou hast made Thy servant king in place of
my father David, yet I am but a little child; I do not know how to go out
or come in. And Thy servant is in the midst of thy people which Thou hast chosen, a
great people who cannot be numbered or counted for multitude.
So give Thy servant an understanding heart to judge Thy people to discern between
good and evil. For who is able to judge this great people of Thine?" 1 Kings 3:7-9

Shortly after King Solomon had asked the Lord for wisdom, two harlots brought their case before him.

Each woman stated that one particular infant belonged to her. Obviously one of them was lying. You see, one woman's child had died shortly after his birth and she had taken the other woman's live baby, laying her dead son in the other mother's arms.

As they stood arguing and shouting, Solomon said, " 'Get me a sword.' So they brought a sword before the king. And the king said, 'Divide the living child in two, and give half to the one and half to the other' " (1 Kings 3:24-25). Solomon knew that the child's true mother would come to the baby's defense.

Within minutes the issue was resolved and the real mother held her child again. "When all Israel heard of the judgment which the king had handed down, they feared the king; for they saw that the wisdom of God was in him to administer justice" (1 Kings 3:28).

{ PRAYER }

Lord, how I pray that such wisdom
would be given to lawmakers.
I also need Your guidance for my family.
Help me remember to turn to You
in my dilemmas.

peace despite our trials

Therefore, having been justified by faith, we have peace with God
through our Lord Jesus Christ, through whom also we have obtained
our introduction by faith into this grace in which we stand;
and we exult in hope of the glory of God. . . . For while we were still helpless,
at the right time Christ died for the ungodly. Romans 5:1-2, 6

People have scoured every nook and cranny of the globe in search of peace. From yoga and transcendental meditation to new age tranquility tapes and self-empowerment courses, people will try just about anything. But do these methods work?

Of course not! Instead, each new road eventually leads to the dead ends of dissatisfaction and emptiness. "I have seen all the works which have been done under the sun, and behold, all is vanity and striving after the wind" (Ecclesiastes 1:14). The promises of peace which this world has to offer are nothing more than vapors of an expensive fragrance.

Enduring tranquility cannot be found outside a relationship with Christ. So why can't we just believe it's that simple?

Maybe we're simply afraid to end the search. Before I became a Christian

I can recall thinking of God as my "ace in the hole." If all else failed, I'd try religion. And when all the other inlets I traveled led to dry lake beds, I did reach out for religion. However, this too was but an attempt on my part to "be good enough for God." Human effort doesn't bring peace.

{ P R A Y E R }

Lord, I know the only true and lasting peace
comes from Jesus Christ.

the content of our thoughts

Woe to those who scheme iniquity, Who work out evil on their beds!
When morning comes, they do it, For it is in the power of their hands.
They covet fields and then seize them, And houses, and take them away.
They rob a man and his house, a man and his inheritance. Micah 2:1-2

Micah acknowledges that the source of evil thoughts is the human mind. Other portions of Scripture also bear out this truth.

"Transgression speaks to the ungodly within his heart; There is no fear of God before his eyes. For it flatters him in his own eyes, Concerning the discovery of his iniquity and the hatred of it. The words of his mouth are wickedness and deceit; He has ceased to be wise and do good. He plans wickedness upon his bed; He sets himself on a path that is not good; He does not despise evil" (Psalm 36:1-4).

Therein lies the problem that we at some point begin to accept wickedness as good. And the things we devise in our minds then become the vehicle for our actions.

Part and parcel of idolatrous worship, for which Israel as a nation assumed guilt before God, was that of human sacrifice to pagan gods. Can you understand why this sin was so detestable to the Lord?

Lord, guard my mind from evil that I might not ruminate
on such things and be propelled into ungodly actions.
Instead, let me turn to Your Word which acts as a cleansing agent.

how to know if you're in love

"Although we love each other deeply, I know there will be times when we'll fail to be there for one another. That's when we'll go to the Lord to receive in abundance what we lack." These words of wisdom were spoken by a twenty-four-year-old woman who had just become engaged. If only more marriages began this way! For even though we've prayed for godly mates, and then relied on His guidance, there will still be times when our attempts to love are less than perfect.

However, if both man and woman turn back to God's blueprint, harmony can be restored. "Love is patient, love is kind, and is not jealous; love does not brag and is not arrogant, does not act unbecomingly; it does not seek its own, is not provoked, does not take into account a wrong suffered, does not rejoice in unrighteousness, but rejoices with the truth; bears all things, believes all things, hopes all things, endures all things. Love never fails" (1 Corinthians 13:4-8).

Why don't more people tap into this resource? To truly love someone means that we will always place that person's welfare above our own. This, after all, is how God loves us.

{ PRAYER }

Lord, help me exhibit true love.

when will our suffering end?

Blessed be the God and Father of our Lord Jesus Christ,
the Father of mercies and God of all comfort; who comforts us
in all our affliction so that we may be able to comfort those
who are in any affliction with the comfort with which
we ourselves are comforted by God. But if we are afflicted,
it is for your comfort and salvation. 2 Corinthians 1:3-4, 6

An experienced mountain biker and triathelete, my son hit some debris in the street when he was riding recently and, before he could dislodge his shoe clips, was thrown from his bike and onto a pile of bricks. His knee took the brunt of the fall, requiring surgery to repair the breaks.

Yet he seems to be taking this whole episode in stride, with a graciousness one wouldn't think possible. He and his fiancée have learned to depend upon each other in a new way: She is providing the medical expertise he desperately needs, while he has learned to allow her to intervene. And both of them depend entirely on the Lord's sufficiency.

This is the purpose of our trials, that we might comfort one another and lean on the Lord's strength. Paul's own burdens had been borne with a view of Christ that few of us will ever know.

Thank You, God,
that in heaven all suffering will cease.

a husband's love

Wives, be subject to your own husbands, as to the Lord.
For the husband is the head of the wife, as Christ also is the head
of the church, He Himself being the Savior of the body.
But as the church is subject to Christ, so also the wives ought
to be to their husbands in everything. Ephesians 5:22-24

Wives, our role is that of a helpmate, not a doormat. It's critical to remember that God intended marriage to be a partnership. Thus, if each person vies for control, the union begins eroding until it simply dissolves. Instead, we need to build one another up.

"So husbands ought also to love their own wives as their own bodies. He who loves his own wife loves himself; for no one ever hated his own flesh, but nourishes and cherishes it, just as Christ also does the church, because we are members of His body" (Ephesians 5:28-29). If men truly loved their wives to this degree, there probably isn't a woman alive who'd run from it.

So what can we do to make things better? Pray. . .every single day. But especially when things are out of kilter. Know that God is vitally interested in the success of your marriage and act accordingly.

Lord, I know that only You are capable of loving perfectly.
So the next time my marriage feels like a 90/10 proposition,
please remind me that You're giving 100 percent.

christ removes ethnic barriers

There is no distinction between Greek and Jew, circumcised and uncircumcised, barbarian, Scythian, slave and freeman, but Christ is all, and in all. And so, as those who have been chosen of God, holy and beloved, put on a heart of compassion, kindness, humility, gentleness and patience; bearing with one another; just as the Lord forgave you, so also should you. Colossians 3:11-13

To say we love Christ and yet maintain deeply rooted prejudices against others is inconsistent with everything He taught. For Christ came to reconcile all peoples to Himself, not separate us into factions.

Above all, God wants us to be harmonious in worship of Him and also in working with Him. "Now may the God who gives perseverance and encouragement grant you to be of the same mind with one another according to Christ Jesus; that with one accord you may with one voice glorify the God and Father of our Lord Jesus Christ. Wherefore, accept one another, just as Christ also accepted us to the glory of God" (Romans 15:5-7).

{ PRAYER }

Lord, let the true peace of Christmas,
which is Christ, be found in my heart
as I am obedient to Your command
to love one another, just as You have loved me
(John 13:34).

If you enjoyed this book, look for the best-selling
Daily Wisdom for Women
wherever books are sold.

© 2003 by Barbour Publishing, Inc.

ISBN 1-58660-700-6

Scripture taken from the New American Standard Bible, ©1960, 1962, 1963, 1968,
1971, 1972, 1973, 1975, 1977 by the Lockman Foundation. Used by permission.

Cover image ©Neovision Europe/Photonica
Pages 20–21 ©Special Photographers Comp/Photonica
Book design by Kevin Keller| designconcepts

Published by Barbour Books, an imprint of Barbour Publishing, Inc.,
P.O. Box 719, Uhrichsville, Ohio 44683 www.barbourbooks.com

Printed in China.
5 4 3 2 1